Vedado, Havana's Forbidden Neighborhood

A TRAVEL PHOTO ART BOOK

LAINE CUNNINGHAM

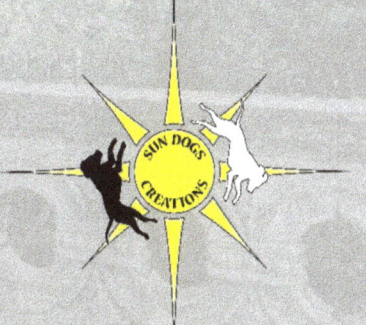

Vedado, Havana's Forbidden Neighborhood
A Travel Photo Art Book

Published by Sun Dogs Creations
Changing the World One Book at a Time
Print ISBN: 978-1-951389-34-5

Cover Image by Laine Cunningham
Cover Design by Angel Leya

Copyright © 2024 Laine Cunningham

All rights reserved. No part of this book may be reproduced in any form or by any means, electronic, mechanical, digital, photocopying or recording, except for the inclusion in a review, without permission in writing from the publisher.

Originally developed as a military zone in the mid-1800s, and therefore inaccessible to average citizens, Vedado was transformed by the sugar trade. The homes in this neighborhood are unique examples of Cuban architecture. While many have been subdivided to accommodate more families, a number are used as hotels, museums, and government offices.

Restaurants in Vedado add international flare to the food culture. The vivid arts venues range from jazz clubs to artist coops. The streets remain peaceful, making the area one of the safest in Havana. Visitors enjoy easy access to the Malécon and the stunning Colon Cemetery.

Walk, bike, or ride along 23rd Street, including La Rampa, to connect with the most popular places to relax. Cruise the Avenida de los Presidentes for historical monuments. Be sure to try Paseo for architectural highlights lining a green boulevard. Begin your journey with *Vedado, Havana's Forbidden Neighborhood.*

MEMORY

RAVEL

DIVERGENCE

AQUATIC

AUSTERITY

CHECKERBOARD

NAZAR

SKIRMISH

TYPEFACE

DRAPERY

ABATE

CRUISE SHIP

ALGAL

DRIFT

FRONTAGE

GRUB HUB

CHIC

SNOWDRIFT

CHIFFON

WELKIN

AWAIT

ECHELON

MARINE

ORGANIC

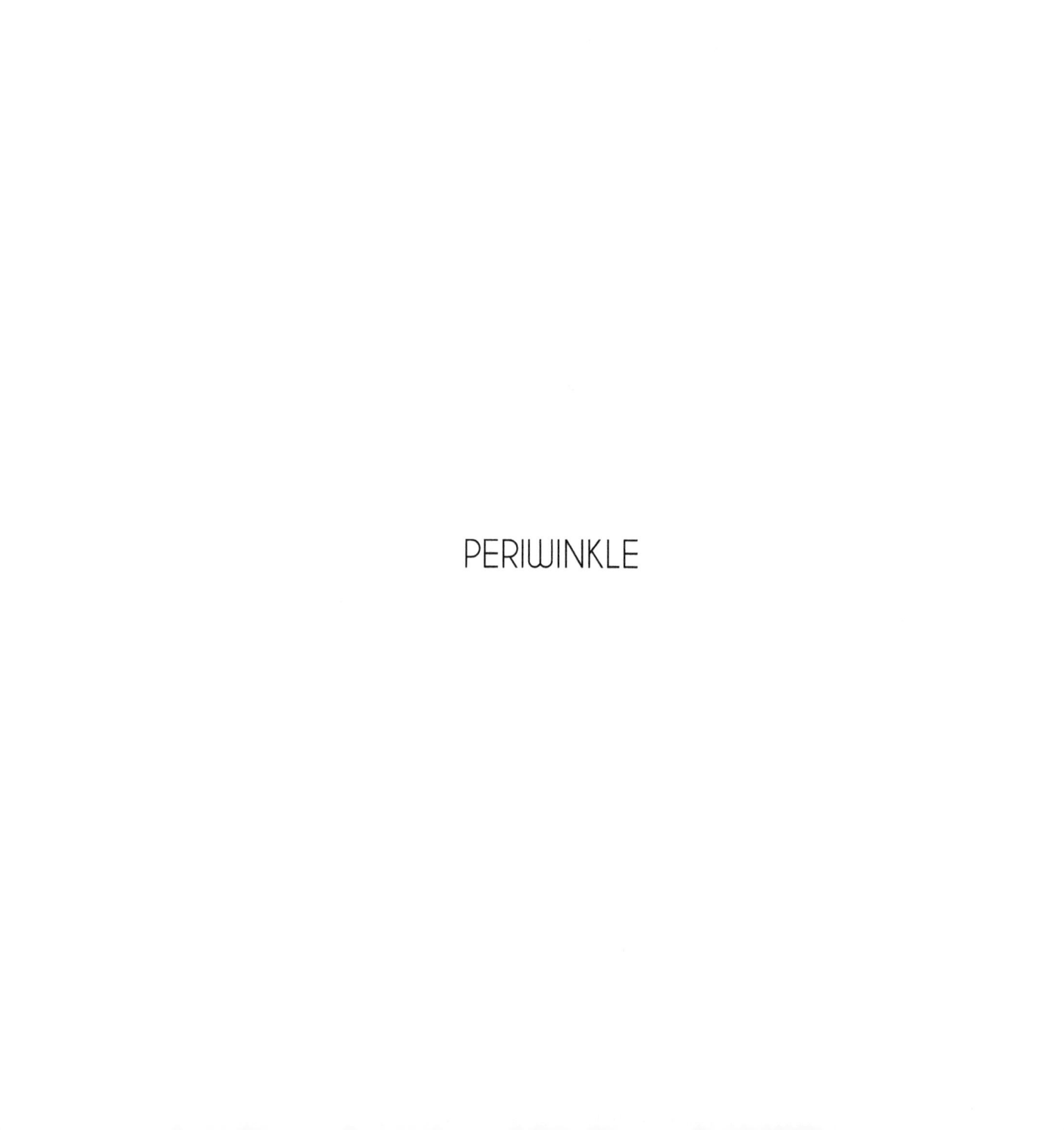

REGENERATE

QUAKE

HELADO

DOMINOES

MATURATION

PANTONE

FORELAND

PYLON

ONGOING

SCOPE

SHIFT

SHOULDER

RESPITE

PREGÓN

THIRST

DOCKING

CONSUMMATION

TITLES IN THIS SERIES

Havana, Cuba
Old Havana, Cuba, the City of Columns
The Malecón, Havana, Cuba
Central Havana, Cuba
Vedado, Havana's Forbidden Neighborhood
Regla, the Quieter Side of Havana, Cuba
Miramar, Havana, Cuba
Streets of Havana, Cuba
Classic Cars of Cuba
Classic Cars of Old Havana, Cuba
Classic Cars of Havana, Cuba
Spanish Colonial Havana, Cuba
Gardens of Havana, Cuba
Verge Gardens of Havana, Cuba
Cats of Havana, Cuba
Colón Cemetery, Cuba
National Art Schools of Havana, Cuba

www.ingramcontent.com/pod-product-compliance
Lightning Source LLC
Chambersburg PA
CBHW040002080526
44586CB00027B/2851